THE Christian's GUIDE TO Passover

Judah Thomas

THE Christian's GUIDE TO Passover

© Judah Thomas 2015

All rights reserved. Without limiting the rights under copyright reserved above, no part of this publication may be reproduced, stored in a retrieval system, or transmitted, in any form or by any means (electronic, mechanical, photocopying, recording or otherwise), without the prior written permission of the copyright owner of this book.

Scripture quotations are taken from the Holy Bible, New Living Translation, copyright ©1996, 2004, 2007, 2013 by Tyndale House Foundation. Used by permission of Tyndale House Publishers, Inc., Carol Stream, Illinois 60188. All rights reserved.

Published by
Meatloaf Media LLC
32 Zwicks Farm Rd
Plantsville, CT 06479
www.meatloafmedia.com

Table of Contents

INTRODUCTION 2
How to Use This Guide 4
Preparation 5
Haroset Recipe 6

THE PASSOVER MEAL 7
Chametz Removal 8
First Cup - Sactification 9
Washing of the Hands 10
Dipping the Parsley 11
Breaking of the Middle Matzah 12
The Four Questions 13
The Passover Story 14
Second Cup - Deliverance 16
It Would Have Been Enough 17
The Bone 18
The Unleavened Bread 19
The Bitter Herbs 20
The Haroset 21
The Egg 22
The Afikoman 23
Third Cup - Redemption 24
Fourth Cup - Praise 25
Elijah's Cup 26
Come Lord Jesus 27

Introduction

The Passover is one of the oldest celebrated holidays in the history of mankind, the only holiday that is older is the celebration of the New Year. Passover was first celebrated by the Jewish people before their escape out of slavery. God gave specific instructions in Exodus 12 for how to celebrate this holiday and told them that they were to celebrate it for all time.

Most Christians find great significance in observing Christmas and Easter but often will overlook Passover. They may feel that it isn't relevant to them or they simply don't understand it. Either way it is important to realize that this is a holiday that Jesus celebrated and was in fact the last meal that he had with his disciples.

We will often celebrate the Lord's Supper or Communion but we fail to realize that this act of remembrance is actually embedded into the Passover feast. The bread and wine was already an important aspect of Passover long before Jesus gave the disciples a new meaning for these elements they were consuming.

I was raised in a Christian home but we never celebrated Passover and so I never truly understood its importance. Several years ago I was inspired to celebrate the Passover with my family as a way to understand Jesus and his sacrifice better. I never realized how difficult it would be to celebrate a holiday that we had no history with.

Honestly, our first Passover probably didn't look very accurate to someone who has been celebrating it their whole life. But it brought my family a new understanding of the sacrifice that Jesus made and how God had planned it since the beginning of time. It brought a new realization of what Communion really is and how Jesus was truly becoming our Passover lamb as is mentioned in 1 Corinthians 5:7.

Christ, our Passover Lamb, has been sacrificed for us. <u>1 Corinthians 5:7c</u>

While we were trying to learn how to have Passover I was overwhelmed with the Haggadah, which is the Jewish text that sets the order for the Seder meal. Many of them were long and my children would lose interest pretty quickly. Over the years I have worked to make a practical Haggadah that reflects the Jewish traditions but also includes the truth about Jesus. I hope that this guide will help you to have a successful Seder dinner and that it will help you appreciate Jesus and his sacrifice in a whole new way.

How to Use This Guide

The Seder is the traditional meal that is celebrated during Passover and tells the story of Exodus. We have provided the basics for hosting a Seder dinner for your family or friends. You can provide each with a copy of this guide for participation or the leader can simply read all the parts and guide everyone else.

I suggest that you read through the entirety of this guide before hosting a Seder meal to familiarize yourself with all of the elements. This can be a rather complex holiday to celebrate and I have done my best to break it down into the simplest form. As you read this you may feel like it still isn't very simple, but trust me when I say that this is far simpler than most.

Keep in mind that the Seder itself is not a meal but is celebrated throughout the course of a meal. In addition to the Seder preparations you will want to prepare a simple meal of chicken, lamb or something along those lines. If you have small children keep in mind that this meal can last between 30 to 60 minutes (traditionally it can last much longer).

Preparation

The Seder meal will require a bit of preparation, and if you have never celebrated Passover before much of it will be unfamiliar to you. I have tried to make things as simple as possible so that your first Seder will be easy and meaningful.

You will need a plate for each person which the Seder elements will be placed on. Often the leader will have a ceremonial Seder plate for their use, but that is optional.

For Leader

- 2 white candles
- 3 squares of matzah wrapped in a large fabric napkin
- Small reward (money, toy or candy)
- Roasted bone (often lamb or chicken)

For Each Person

- Sprig of parsley
- Spoonful of haroset
- Wine glasses
- Wine or grape juice (each person will get four servings)
- Bowl of saltwater (these can be shared)
- Spoonful of horseradish
- Matzah
- Boiled egg
- (Optional) Romaine lettuce as the other bitter herb

Traditionally you will also create one extra place setting for Elijah.

Haroset

Haroset is a traditional apple relish that is used to remind us of the mortar that was used by the Israelites to contruct the Egyptian cities.

Ingredients

Mix together the following ingredients

- 2 large apples - peeled, cored and finely chopped
- 1 cup walnuts - finely chopped
- 1 teaspoon ground cinnamon
- 1 teaspoon sugar
- 2 tablespoons wine or grape juice

The Passover Meal

Chametz Removal

Chametz is any food that has been leavened such as bread and it is removed as a symbol of removing impurities. This is basically a scavenger hunt where the children will find any bread in the house and remove it. We generally put it in a plastic bag and place it outside for the duration of the meal. For the reading you can substitute the word "bread" for "chametz" if you prefer.

(Once the chametz has been removed from the home, gather around the table for the blessing.)

Prayer:

Blessed are you, our God, Creator of the universe who makes us holy and commanded us to remove the chametz. Any chametz, which is in our possession that we did not see, which we did not remove, will be nullified and be ownerless as the dust of the earth.

Blessed are you, our God, Creator of the universe who makes us holy and commanded us to light festival candles. You have given us life, sustained us, and enabled us to reach this season of Joy. Amen.

(Light the candles.)

First Cup - Sanctification

(Fill all of the cups with wine or juice. Do not overfill because each person will be getting four servings.)

Leader:
This first cup is the cup of sanctification. Sanctification simply means "to be set apart for God." Just as the Jews were set apart we are also set apart by God.

<u>1 Peter 2:9</u> But you are not like that, for you are a chosen people. You are royal priests, a holy nation, God's very own possession. As a result, you can show others the goodness of God, for he called you out of the darkness into his wonderful light.

(Raise your glass and bless the first cup.)

Prayer:
Blessed are you, our God, Creator of the universe who created the fruit of the vine. You have chosen us, made us holy, and set us apart so we can show others your goodness. You have kept us alive, sustained us, and brought us to this season. Amen.

(Everyone drinks the first cup.)

Washing of the Hands

(Each person washes their hands in a basin with water or simply at the sink.)

Leader:

We wash our hands to remember how the priests would wash their hands before they could come before God. We realize that pointed to Jesus who is the one that washes our sins away. We also remember when Jesus took on the role of a servant and washed the disciples feet before their last Passover meal.

Dipping the Parsley

(Everyone takes their sprig of parsley and dips it into the salt water two times.)

Leader:

We will dip our sprig of parsley into the salt water two times.

(Dip the sprig into the salt water.)

The first time is to remember the tears that the Israelites shed while in slavery.

(Dip the sprig into the salt water again.)

The second time is to remember how God saved the Israelites by drowning the Egyptian army in the Red Sea.

Prayer:

Blessed are you our God, Creator of the universe who creates the fruit of the earth. Amen

(Everyone eats or takes a bite of the sprig of parsley.)

Breaking of the Middle Matzah

(Uncover the stack of three matzah. Break the middle one in half when talking about Jesus' body.)

Leader:
In these pieces of matzah we can see the Trinity. The top piece represents God the Father, the bottom piece represents the Holy Spirit and the middle one represents the Son Jesus whose body was broken for us and wrapped in a cloth the placed in a tomb.

Mark 15:46 Joseph bought a long sheet of linen cloth. Then he took Jesus' body down from the cross, wrapped it in the cloth, and laid it in a tomb that had been carved out of the rock. Then he rolled a stone in front of the entrance.

(Put one broken piece back into the middle of the stack and wrap the other one with the cloth and then hide it somewhere in the house while everyone closes their eyes.)

The Four Questions

(Pour the second cup of juice or wine but do not drink it yet. Then have the youngest child or the youngest person present ask the following questions.)

Youngest:
Why is this night different from all other nights?

Leader:
In what ways do you find this night different?

Youngest:
This night is different in four ways.

1. **ON ALL OTHER NIGHTS we may eat chametz (bread) but on this night we eat matzah.**

2. **ON ALL OTHER NIGHTS we may eat many vegetables, but on this night we eat parsley**

3. **ON ALL OTHER NIGHTS we don't dip even once, but on this night we dip twice.**

4. **ON ALL OTHER NIGHTS we eat sitting up or reclining, but on this night we all recline.**

The Passover Story

Leader:

Long ago in the land of Egypt, Joseph was sold into slavery by his brothers. God blessed Joseph with the ability to interpret dreams and became an Egyptian official and Pharaoh's second in command. Joseph had predicted a famine and helped the Egyptians to prepare in advance. Joseph's family came to Egypt to live during this famine.

Many years later a new Pharaoh came into power and instead of living peacefully with the Israelites he forced them into slavery. For 400 years the Israelites were slaves to the Egyptians.

The Israelites grew in number and strength and the Pharaoh commanded all baby boys to be drowned in the river. A young boy was born to a slave couple who put him in a basket in the river. When Pharaoh's daughter came to the river to bathe she found the basket and decided to keep the boy. She named him Moses, which means, "brought out of the water."

Moses lived a rich life in the Pharaoh's palace but could not bear watching his people living in slavery. One day Moses saw an Egyptian beating a slave and in a fit of rage he beat the taskmaster to death. Moses fled for his life into the wilderness where he lived for forty years.

One day when Moses was tending his sheep God spoke to him through a bush that was burning but was not consumed. God's voice told Moses to go back to Egypt to free the Israelites from slavery. Moses was reluctant to go but God assured Moses that He would be by his side.

Moses returned to Egypt with his brother Aaron and went to see the Pharaoh and demanded, "Let my people go!" But the Pharaoh had a hard heart and would not let them go. Through Moses, God brought ten plagues upon the Egyptians. Several times Pharaoh promised to let the people go, but then went back on his word.

Let My People Go

Verse 1
When Israel was in Egypt's land
Let My people Go
Oppressed so hard they could not stand
Let My people Go

Go Down Moses, way down in Egypt's land
Tell old Pharaoh, Let my people go

Verse 2
So Moses went to Egypt's land
Let my people go
To make old Pharaoh understand
Let my people go

Go Down Moses, way down in Egypt's land
Tell old Pharaoh, Let my people go

Leader:
After the ninth plague God warned that He would bring one more plague upon Egypt. He told them that a Death Angel would pass through Egypt and that every firstborn in the land would die.

God instructed Moses to tell the Israelites to sacrifice a lamb and to take the blood from the lamb and sprinkle it on the doorpost of their homes. They were to roast the lamb and eat it with unleavened bread and bitter herbs.

That night the Death Angel went throughout Egypt and killed every firstborn as promised. However, the plague "passed over" the homes of the Israelites. After this last plague the Pharaoh finally freed the Israelites.

Second Cup - Deliverance

Leader:
This is the Cup of Deliverance because God promised to deliver the Israelites from the bondage of Egypt. We will now take our finger and dip it into the wine (juice) and let a drop for each plague fall onto our plate as we all say the ten plagues.

1. Blood
2. Frogs
3. Lice
4. Flies
5. Livestock Disease
6. Boils
7. Hail
8. Locusts
9. Darkness
10. Death of the firstborn

After the plagues the Israelites quickly packed their belongings and Moses led them into the desert. Once again the Pharaoh changed his mind and tried to capture the Israelites.

The Egyptian army trapped the Israelites at the Red Sea and God told Moses to hold out his wooden staff. A strong wind began to blow and the Red Sea parted and allowed the freed slaves to cross unharmed. The Egyptian soldiers tried to follow the Israelites across but Moses once again held up his staff and the waters closed killing the Egyptian army.

At last the Israelites were free!

It Would Have Been Enough

Leader: If God had brought us out of Egypt, but not carried out judgements against the Egyptians.
All: It would have been enough.

Leader: If God had carried out judgements against the Egyptians, but not against their idols.
All: It would have been enough.

Leader: If God had destroyed their idols, but not killed their firstborn.
All: It would have been enough.

Leader: If God had killed their firstborn, but not given us their wealth.
All: It would have been enough.

Leader: If God had given us their wealth, but not split the Sea for us.
All: It would have been enough.

Leader: If God had split the Sea for us, but not led us through it on dry land.
All: It would have been enough.

Leader: If God had led us through it on dry land, but not drowned our oppressors in it.
All: It would have been enough.

Leader: If God had drowned our oppressors in it, but not provided our needs in the desert for forty years.
All: It would have been enough.

Leader: If God had provided our needs in the desert for forty years, but not fed us the manna.
All: It would have been enough.

Leader: If God had fed us the manna, but not given us the Sabbath.
All: It would have been enough.

Leader: If God had given us the Sabbath, but not brought us to Mount Sinai.
All: It would have been enough.

Leader: If God had brought us to Mount Sinai, but not given us the Torah.
All: It would have been enough.

Leader: If God had given us the Torah, but not brought us to the land of Israel.
All: It would have been enough.

Leader: If God had brought us to the land of Israel, but not built the Temple.
All: It would have been enough.

Prayer:

Thank you God, for all the blessings you have given us. You led us out of slavery in Egypt and brought us into the Promised Land. You turned our sorrow into joy. We thank you for the freedom you have given us. Blessed are you, our God, Creator of the universe who created the fruit of the vine. Amen.

(Drink the second cup and have the person sitting next to you refill it.)

The Bone

(Hold up the bone for all to see.)

Leader:

This bone reminds us of the unblemished male lamb that was killed for the first Passover meal. The blood was sprinkled on the doorposts so the firstborn would be spared.

John 1:29 The next day John saw Jesus coming toward him and said, "Look! The Lamb of God who takes away the sin of the world!

The Unleavened Bread

(Hold up the stack of matzah.)

Leader:
We now take this unleavened bread as was commanded by God.

<u>Exodus 34:18a</u> "You must celebrate the Festival of Unleavened Bread. For seven days the bread you eat must be made without yeast, just as I commanded you.

We eat it to remember the Israelites who ate unleavened bread because they did not have time to let it rise. They were forced to eat it in the form of hard flat crackers.

Prayer:
Blessed are you, our God, Creator of the universe who gives us bread from the earth. Who made us holy by Your commandments and instructed us to eat the unleavened bread.

(Break a piece of the top two pieces of matzah and pass it around for everyone to eat.)

The Bitter Herbs

(Each person takes a small spoonful of horseradish and/or romaine lettuce, and places it on their matzah.)

Leader:

These bitter herbs remind us of the bitterness of slavery.

Exodus 1:14 They made their lives bitter, forcing them to mix mortar and make bricks and do all the work in the fields. They were ruthless in all their demands.

It also reminds us of the bitterness of our slavery to sin.

John 8:34 Jesus replied, "I tell you the truth, everyone who sins is a slave of sin.

Prayer:

Blessed are you, our God, Creator of the universe who made us holy and has instructed us to eat the bitter herbs.

(Eat the piece of matzah with the bitters herbs.)

Eating the Haroset

(Each person takes a small spoonful of haroset and eats it on their matzah.)

Leader:
This mixture represents the mortar that was used by the Israelites to build the Pharaoh's cities. It is sweet because even labor is sweetened with a promise of redemption.

(If you want you can also mix the bitter herbs with the haroset to taste them both at the same time.)

Sharing the Haroset

(Everyone prepares another piece of matzah with haroset to share with the person next to them.)

Leader:
Now let us prepare another piece of matzah with haroset to share with our neighbor. We share this with our neighbor as a sign of affection and say "Peace be with you."

John 13:26 Jesus responded, "It is the one to whom I give the bread I dip in the bowl." And when he had dipped it, he gave it to Judas, son of Simon Iscariot.

The Egg

(Hold up the egg.)

Leader:
Since the destruction of the temple the Jews were no longer able to offer the sacrifice. The egg is a reminder to us of the sacrifice that was made during ancient times. We now realize that the sacrifice of Jesus cleansed our sins once and for all.

<u>Hebrews 10:10</u> *For God's will was for us to be made holy by the sacrifice of the body of Jesus Christ, once for all time.*

The Meal

(If you are doing the Seder as a full meal the main course can now be eaten. The meal traditionally consists of the boiled egg, roasted lamb, chicken, fish, matzo ball soup, rice, noodles and etc. You can have whatever beverage you want but do not drink from the third cup yet.)

The Afikoman

After the meal the children go and look for the Afikoman, pronounced ah-fee-koh-mun. You can use "hotter and colder" as a way to help them if they have difficulty finding it. Whoever finds it receives a monetary prize or piece of candy as a "ransom."

(Unwrap and hold up the Afikoman.)

Leader:

This matzah was broken which reminds us of Jesus' crucifixion, it was hidden which reminds us of His burial, and now was brought back which reminds us of His Resurrection.

Looking closely at the unleavened bread. We see the holes that remind us of what we are told in Isaiah 53:5. "He was pierced for our rebellion, crushed for our sins."

The dark marks remind us of the bruises that were on Jesus' body when "He was beaten so we could be whole."

The long lines remind us of the stripes on His back when "He was whipped so we could be healed."

During the Last Supper, Jesus used this piece of unleavened as a symbol of His sacrifice.

Luke 22:19 *He took some bread and gave thanks to God for it. Then he broke it in pieces and gave it to the disciples, saying, "This is my body, which is given for you. Do this to remember me."*

(Break the Afikoman and hand a piece to everyone to eat.)

Third Cup
- Redemption

(Hold up the cup of wine or juice.)

Leader:

The Jews would use this cup to symbolize the blood of the Passover lamb. God had redeemed them and had brought them out of slavery. We remember that Jesus is the one that redeems us from the bondage of sin.

<u>Luke 1:68</u> "Praise the Lord, the God of Israel, because he has visited and redeemed his people.

As we drink this Cup of Redemption let's remember that Jesus has become our redemption.

(Have each person refill the glass of the person sitting next to them.)

Fourth Cup - Praise

(Raise the glass of wine or juice.)

Leader:

This Cup of Praise reminds us of the many things God has done for us. Let us give thanks and praise to God.

<u>Psalm 150</u> Praise the Lord! Praise God in his sanctuary; praise him in his mighty heaven!

2 Praise him for his mighty works; praise his unequaled greatness!

3 Praise him with a blast of the ram's horn; praise him with the lyre and harp!

4 Praise him with the tambourine and dancing; praise him with strings and flutes!

5 Praise him with a clash of cymbals; praise him with loud clanging cymbals.

6 Let everything that breathes sing praises to the Lord!
Praise the Lord!

Prayer:
Blessed are you, our God, Creator of the universe who created the fruit of the vine.

Elijah's Cup

(Pour wine or juice into the cup set aside for Elijah. You can either pass this cup around for everyone to share, they can dip a piece of matzah in it, or you can pour another small amount of wine or juice for each to have their own.)

Leader:

The Israelites would set an extra cup for Elijah, but they would not drink from it because they were waiting for Elijah to come to announce the coming of the Messiah. As the Passover meal was coming to a close Jesus picked up the Cup of Elijah and for the first time drank from this cup and served it to his disciples.

Mark 14:23-24 And he took a cup of wine and gave thanks to God for it. He gave it to them, and they all drank from it. 24 And he said to them, "This is my blood, which confirms the covenant between God and his people. It is poured out as a sacrifice for many.

Come Lord Jesus

Prayer:
Blessed are you, our God, Creator of the universe. We thank you for the Sacrifice that Jesus made for us, giving us the ability to be made right with you. We believe that Jesus alone is Lord of all and has paid the price for our sin on the cross.

<u>Numbers 6:24</u> "The Lord bless you and keep you; 25 the Lord make his face shine on you and be gracious to you; 26 the Lord turn his face toward you and give you peace." Amen.

As we await the Second coming of Christ let us finish our Seder dinner and all say "Come Lord Jesus."

<u>Matthew 26:30</u> Then they sang a hymn and went out to the Mount of Olives.

Let us now sing a song of praise together.

Amazing Grace

Amazing grace! How sweet the sound
That saved a wretch like me!
I once was lost, but now am found;
Was blind, but now I see.

'Twas grace that taught my heart to fear,
And grace my fears relieved;
How precious did that grace appear
The hour I first believed.

Made in the USA
Columbia, SC
10 April 2025